Vegan
Ice Cream
Sandwiches

Vegan
Ice Cream
Sandwiches

{ Cool Recipes for Delicious
Dairy-Free Ice Creams and Cookies }

Kris Holechek Peters

Ulysses Press

Published by
Ulysses Press
P.O. Box 3440
Berkeley, CA 94703
www.ulyssespress.com

ISBN: 978-1-61243-298-4
Library of Congress Catalog Number 2013957413

Printed in the United States by Bang Printing

10 9 8 7 6 5 4 3 2 1

Acquisitions editor: Kelly Reed
Managing editor: Claire Chun
Editor: Lauren Harrison
Proofreader: Elyce Berrigan-Dunlop
Front cover design: Rebecca Lown
Interior design and layout: what!design @ whatweb.com
Cover photograph: © JudySwinksPhotography.com
Food stylist: Anna Hartman-Kenzler
Index: Sayre Van Young

Distributed by Publishers Group West

To J. Cray, for everything, not least of all sharing the wonders of ice cream with me.

Table of Contents

Introduction

Ice cream sandwiches are a melding of two independently delicious treats, but united they are a culinary force to be reckoned with. I mean, come on! Ice cream smooshed between not one, but two cookies? It's like the nectar of the dessert gods. But never fear, the amazing feat of making your own ice cream sandwiches is easy to achieve.

In this book you will find combination after combination of smooth, creamy ice creams, paired with complementary cookies. They will dazzle your taste buds and open the door to many more flavorful pairings as you mix and match the recipes to your heart's desire.

Ice cream sandwiches are a great little treat to bring out on warm days, or to tuck in the freezer to impress your guests after a lovely meal.

So enjoy, have fun, and make sure you taste the ice cream and cookies each step of the way. You know, quality control.

Making Vegan Ice Cream

Ten years ago, the idea of vegan ice cream seemed far-fetched and nearly impossible. Ice cream without the cream? But over the past decade more and more nondairy ice cream companies have been taking over freezer cases in grocery stores across the country and have made it clear that not only is vegan ice cream possible, but it's also delicious.

In this book, you'll find ice creams made from three different bases: soy, coconut, and raw cashew. I find that different bases play better to certain flavors, but also they provide more flexibility if you are making dessert for someone who has food allergies. No one should be excluded from the ice cream sandwich magic.

Making ice cream at home is very easy, but does require advance planning. Take time to read the instructions for your ice cream maker so it is ready to use when the mood strikes. Recipes need to be initially cooked then cooled down at least to room temperature before being put in the ice cream maker, so plan accordingly. Additionally, the ice cream will need to set in the freezer for a while (ideally at least 2 hours) after being processed in the ice cream maker before it can be eaten. With those things taken into consideration, the actual active time making ice cream is minimal.

Depending on how much ice cream you pack between your cookies and how big the cookies are, you might end up with extra ice cream from the recipes. This, my friends, is what we call a *good* problem. I'm sure you'll find a way to use it up.

One of the best parts of making your own ice cream sandwiches is that you are in control: If you want bite-sized treats, make the cookies half the size and you'll double your yield. Want fun shapes? Bust out those cookie cutters and get cutting. Additionally, you can mix and match the different ice creams and cookies to make endless combinations (or 1,770 combinations, which is still, you know, *a lot*).

Ingredients and Tools

There are some staple tools and ingredients used in this book that you'll want to have for a well-stocked kitchen.

Ice Cream Maker: These recipes depend on having an ice cream maker. Thankfully, there are some very inexpensive models that will serve you just fine. They are also a frequently purchased but seldom used appliance for many people, so you can likely find a great deal on a used model on Craigslist.

Milks: Remember, we are replacing cream here, so fat content counts. It keeps the ice cream from getting those icy shards in it and is essential for the mouthfeel.

- **Soy Milk:** You can also use a higher-fat nondairy milk such as hemp milk here, but be sure to use regular versions, not fat-free.

- **Coconut Milk:** We're talking about the good, old-fashioned cans of coconut milk, not the coconut beverage that has been taking over grocery stores for the past few years. Fat is your friend, at least in making ice cream, and coconut milk is a good friend to have.

- **Raw Cashews:** Raw nuts have a more delicate flavor and are also softer than roasted nuts, making them perfect for rich and creamy ice cream bases. Cashews are preferable, but you could also try raw almonds, with the skins removed, or if you want to be over-the-top decadent, macadamia nuts.

Guar Gum: This is a natural, plant-based thickener that you've probably seen on the back of many a food label. It's much easier to find than it used to be due to its usefulness in gluten-free baking. It can seem a little spendy, but you use so little that one bag will last you a long time.

Starch: Tapioca or arrowroot starch are great tools for thickening up liquids and are friends to ice cream, helping it maintain a smooth mouthfeel. You'll see both used throughout the book. They hold up in frozen goods much better than their friend cornstarch.

Coconut Oil: Coconut oil is thick and rich, helping us get the proper amount of fat in our ice cream.

Aseptic Tofu: This is the tofu that comes in the airtight containers. It's shelf-stable and usually contains about 12 ounces of tofu. This is often called "silken tofu," which is great due to its über-creamy consistency.

Plastic Wrap: Plastic wrap is really the best option for wrapping up the sandwiches before freezing them. The ice cream will have more of a soft-serve consistency when it's being assembled, so wrapping the sandwiches keeps everything together while they firm up and also prevents freezer burn. I like to wrap each sandwich in plastic wrap, then tuck them into waxed paper sandwich bags. Then, I fold over the bag and secure it with a sticker labeled with the type of sandwich that's inside. It makes for a beautiful presentation and also helps you remember which 'wich is which.

Food Processor or High-Speed Blender (optional but awesome): Some of the recipes, particularly the nut-based ones, rely on some sort of appliance that can blend the ice cream base into a smooth consistency.

Recipes

Classic
Ice Cream Sandwiches

The essential sandwich in any ice cream sandwich arsenal is the classic chocolate cookie, bookending a simple vanilla ice cream.

Makes: 12 to 16 sandwiches

Classic Chocolate Cookies

Makes: about 2 dozen cookies

⅓ cup nondairy margarine, at room temperature
⅔ cup evaporated cane sugar
2 tablespoons nondairy milk
¼ teaspoon mild vinegar
1 teaspoon vanilla extract
¾ cup unbleached all-purpose flour
⅓ cup unsweetened baking cocoa, sifted
½ teaspoon baking powder
⅛ teaspoon salt

1 } Preheat the oven to 375°F. Line a baking sheet with parchment paper.

2 } In a medium bowl, cream together the margarine and sugar. Stir in the milk, vinegar, and vanilla. In a small bowl, combine the flour, cocoa, baking powder, and salt. Add the dry ingredients to the wet and mix thoroughly.

3 } Turn out onto the prepared baking sheet. Place a sheet of waxed paper over the dough and roll out into a square about ¼ inch thick. Remove the

waxed paper and bake for 10 to 12 minutes, until the edges are set and it's slightly puffy. It will seem soft and not fully baked, but it is.

4} Remove from the oven and let cool for about 15 minutes on the baking sheet on a wire rack. Carefully cut the cookies into the desired shape. You can use a glass or biscuit cutter to make them round, or maximize the dough by cutting them into evenly sized squares.

5} Remove the cookies from the sheet and allow to finish cooling on the rack.

Vanilla Soy Ice Cream

Makes: 1¼ quarts

¾ cup evaporated cane sugar
1 tablespoon plus 2 teaspoons tapioca starch
2½ cups soy or hemp milk (full fat)
1 teaspoon coconut oil
2 teaspoons vanilla extract

1} In a large saucepan, combine the sugar and tapioca starch and whisk until incorporated. Pour in the milk, whisking to incorporate. Over medium heat, bring the mixture to a boil, whisking frequently. Once it reaches a boil, lower the heat to medium-low and whisk constantly until the mixture thickens and coats the back of a spoon, about 5 minutes. Remove from the heat, add the coconut oil and vanilla, and mix to combine.

2} Transfer the mixture to a heat-resistant bowl and let it cool completely.

3 } Pour the mixture into the bowl of a 1½- or 2-quart ice cream maker and process according to the manufacturer's instructions. Store in an airtight container in the freezer for at least 2 hours before assembling the sandwiches.

To Make the Sandwiches

1 } Let the ice cream soften slightly so it's easy to scoop. Place half of the cookies, bottoms up, on a clean surface. Scoop one generous scoop of ice cream, about ⅓ cup, onto the top of each cookie. Top the ice cream with the remaining cookies, with the cookie bottoms touching the ice cream. Gently press down on the cookies to level them. Wrap each sandwich in plastic wrap or waxed paper and return to the freezer for at least 30 minutes before serving.

X-Ray
Ice Cream Sandwiches

A play on the classic, just the inverse combination.

Makes: 12 to 16 sandwiches

Vanilla Cookies

Makes: about 2 dozen cookies

2 cups unbleached all-purpose flour
1 teaspoon baking soda
¼ teaspoon salt
1 cup nondairy margarine, at room temperature
½ cup packed brown sugar
½ cup evaporated cane sugar
1 teaspoon cornstarch
2 tablespoons nondairy milk
1½ teaspoons vanilla extract

1} Preheat the oven to 350°F. Line two baking sheets with parchment paper.

2} In a small bowl, combine the flour, baking soda, and salt. In a large bowl, cream together the margarine, brown sugar, and cane sugar. Dissolve the cornstarch in the milk in a small bowl and add to the margarine mixture along with the vanilla. Add the dry ingredients to the wet in batches and mix until smooth.

3 } Using a cookie dropper or tablespoon, drop heaping tablespoons of dough onto the prepared baking sheets about 2 inches apart. Bake for 8 to 10 minutes, or until the edges are slightly golden. Remove from the oven and let cool on the pan for 5 minutes, then remove to cool on a wire rack. Let the cookies cool completely. Store in an airtight container.

Chocolate Soy Ice Cream

Makes: 1¼ quarts

¾ cup evaporated cane sugar
⅓ cup unsweetened baking cocoa, sifted
1 tablespoon tapioca starch
2½ cups soy or hemp milk (full fat)
2 teaspoons coconut oil
2 teaspoons vanilla extract

1 } In a large saucepan, combine the sugar, cocoa, and tapioca starch, and whisk until the cocoa and starch are incorporated into the sugar. Pour in the milk, whisking to incorporate. Over medium heat, bring the mixture to a boil, whisking frequently. Once it reaches a boil, lower the heat to medium-low and whisk constantly until the mixture thickens and coats the back of a spoon, about 5 minutes. Remove from the heat, add the coconut oil and vanilla, and whisk to combine.

2 } Transfer the mixture to a heat-resistant bowl and let it cool completely.

3 } Pour the mixture into the bowl of a 1½- or 2-quart ice cream maker and process according to the manufacturer's instructions. Store in an

airtight container in the freezer for at least 2 hours before assembling the sandwiches.

To Make the Sandwiches

1} Let the ice cream soften slightly so it's easy to scoop. Place half of the cookies, bottoms up, on a clean surface. Scoop one generous scoop of ice cream, about ⅓ cup, onto the top of each cookie. Top the ice cream with the remaining cookies, with the cookie bottoms touching the ice cream. Gently press down on the cookies to level them out. Wrap each sandwich in plastic wrap or waxed paper, and return to the freezer for at least 30 minutes before serving.

Double Chocolate Sandwiches

What's better than chocolate? Double chocolate!

Makes: 12 to 16 sandwiches

Chocolate Cookies

Makes: about 2 dozen cookies

1 cup unbleached all-purpose flour
½ cup unsweetened baking cocoa, sifted
½ teaspoon baking soda
¼ teaspoon salt
¼ cup nondairy chocolate chips, melted
½ cup nondairy margarine, softened
1 cup evaporated cane sugar
1 teaspoon vanilla extract

1} Preheat the oven to 325°F. Line two baking sheets with parchment paper.

2} In a medium bowl, combine the flour, cocoa powder, baking soda, and salt. In a large bowl, with an electric handheld mixer, cream together the melted chocolate chips, margarine, sugar, and vanilla until well combined. Add the dry ingredients to the wet in batches until fully incorporated.

3} Scoop small balls of dough, about the size of a large marble (roughly 2 teaspoons) onto the prepared baking sheets about 2 inches apart. Lightly grease the back of a tablespoon and gently and evenly press down on each cookie until it is flattened and measures about 1½ inches wide. Bake for 12 minutes, or until the edges are set. If you are baking both sheets at the same time, rotate the sheets halfway through.

4} After removing from the oven, let the cookies cool on the pan for 5 minutes, then transfer to a wire rack. Let the cookies cool completely. Store in an airtight container.

Chocolate Coconut Ice Cream

Makes: 1 quart

¾ cup evaporated cane sugar
⅓ cup unsweetened baking cocoa, sifted
1 (13.5-ounce) can full-fat coconut milk (not light)
1 cup nondairy milk
1 teaspoon vanilla extract

1} In a large saucepan, combine the sugar and cocoa, and whisk until the cocoa is incorporated into the sugar. Pour in the coconut milk and the other nondairy milk, whisking to incorporate. Over medium heat, bring the mixture to a boil, whisking frequently. Once it reaches a boil, lower the heat to medium-low and whisk constantly until the sugar is dissolved, about 5 minutes. Remove from the heat and add the vanilla, whisking to combine.

2} Transfer the mixture to a heat-resistant bowl and let it cool completely.

3} Pour the mixture into the bowl of a 1½ or 2-quart ice cream maker and process according to the manufacturer's instructions. Store in an airtight container in the freezer for at least 2 hours before assembling the sandwiches.

To Make the Sandwiches

1 } Let the ice cream soften slightly so it's easy to scoop. Place half of the cookies, bottoms up, on a clean surface. Scoop one generous scoop of ice cream, about ⅓ cup, onto the top of each cookie. Top the ice cream with the remaining cookies, with the cookie bottoms touching the ice cream. Gently press down on the cookies to level them out. Wrap each sandwich in plastic wrap or waxed paper and return to the freezer for at least 30 minutes before serving.

Sandwich Fixin's, Fillin's, and Mixin's

Mix in ½ cup of chopped frozen raspberries or cherries to the ice cream before transferring it to a freezer-safe container for a lovely contrasting flavor.

Strawberry Italiano Sandwiches

This sandwich is perfect for more grown-up palates. The shortbread is crisp and subtle while the balsamic strawberry swirl in the ice cream adds an indescribable tang. In fact, I guarantee you'll like it so much, you'll be making it on its own to smother waffles, pancakes, and other assorted treats.

Makes: 12 to 16 sandwiches

Vanilla Sugar Shortbread Cookies

Makes: about 2 dozen cookies

1 cup nondairy margarine, softened
¾ cup evaporated cane sugar, divided
2 teaspoons vanilla extract
2¼ cups unbleached all-purpose flour

1} In a large bowl, cream together the margarine, ½ cup of the sugar, and the vanilla until well combined. Add the flour in batches and mix until the dough is soft and smooth. Divide the dough in half and shape each half into a rectangular log, about 5 inches long, 3 inches wide, and 2 inches tall. Sprinkle the remaining ¼ cup sugar on a clean surface and roll each log in it to coat the outside. Wrap each log in plastic wrap and refrigerate for at least 2 hours.

2} Preheat the oven to 375°F. Line two baking sheets with parchment paper.

3 } Remove the cookie dough logs from the fridge. Using a sharp knife, cut the logs into ¼-inch-thick slices, pressing the sides of the log as you cut to maintain its shape. Place the sliced cookies on the prepared baking sheets 1 inch apart. Bake for 8 to 10 minutes, or until the edges are lightly browned.

4 } After removing from the oven, let the cookies cool on the pan for 5 minutes, then transfer to a wire rack. Let the cookies cool completely. Store in an airtight container.

Strawberry Balsamic Swirl Coconut Ice Cream

Makes: 1 quart

¾ cup plus 2 tablespoons evaporated cane sugar
1 (13.5-ounce) can full-fat coconut milk (not light)
1 cup nondairy milk
1 teaspoon vanilla extract
½ teaspoon cornstarch or arrowroot starch
¾ cup fresh or frozen and thawed strawberries
1 tablespoon water
2 teaspoons balsamic vinegar

1 } In a large saucepan, combine ¾ cup of the sugar with the coconut and other nondairy milk, whisking to incorporate. Over medium heat, bring the mixture to a boil, whisking frequently. Once it reaches a boil, lower the heat to medium-low and whisk constantly until the sugar is dissolved, about 5 minutes. Remove from the heat and add the vanilla, whisking to combine.

2 } Transfer the mixture to a heat-resistant bowl and let it cool completely.

3 } While the ice cream base is cooking, combine the remaining 2 tablespoons of sugar and starch in a small saucepan. Add the strawberries and water and cook over medium heat, stirring often, until the strawberries are juicy and the mixture begins to bubble, about 5 minutes. Using a potato masher, crush the berries and add the balsamic vinegar. Lower the heat to medium-low and continue cooking, stirring continuously, until the mixture thickens, about 3 minutes, then transfer to a heat-resistant bowl to cool completely.

4 } Pour the ice cream base into the bowl of a 1½- or 2-quart ice cream maker and process according to the manufacturer's instructions. Once the ice cream is ready, scoop one-third into a freezer-safe container, then add half of the cooled strawberry mixture. Add another third of the ice cream and top with the remaining strawberry mixture. Top with the last third of the ice cream, then draw a butter knife through the mixture 2 or 3 times to swirl it. Store in an airtight container in the freezer for at least 2 hours before assembling the sandwiches.

To Make the Sandwiches

1 } Let the ice cream soften slightly so it's easy to scoop. Place half of the cookies, bottoms up, on a clean surface. Scoop one generous scoop of ice cream, about ⅓ cup, onto the top of each cookie. Top the ice cream with the remaining cookies, with the cookie bottoms touching the ice cream. Gently press down the cookies to level them out. Wrap each sandwich in plastic wrap or waxed paper and return to the freezer for at least 30 minutes before serving.

Sandwich Fixin's, Fillin's, and Mixin's

The balsamic swirl can be made with other berries, too. Try this ice cream with a chocolate cookie for another delicious combination.

Carrot Cake
Sandwiches

A soft and fragrant carrot cake cookie surrounds a sweet and slightly spicy ginger ice cream, a welcome twist on the classic cake.

Makes: 12 to 16 sandwiches

Carrot Cake Cookies

Makes: about 2 dozen cookies

2 cups unbleached all-purpose flour
½ teaspoon baking powder
2 teaspoons ground cinnamon
½ teaspoon ground ginger
¼ teaspoon ground nutmeg
¼ teaspoon salt
¾ cup nondairy margarine, at room temperature
1 cup packed dark brown sugar
½ cup evaporated cane sugar
2 teaspoons vanilla extract
1½ cups finely shredded carrots (about 2 medium-large carrots)
⅓ cup toasted, shredded coconut (optional)
⅓ cup crushed walnuts (optional)

1} Preheat the oven to 350°F. Line two baking sheets with parchment paper.

2} In a small bowl, combine the flour, baking powder, cinnamon, ginger, nutmeg, and salt. In a large bowl, cream together the margarine, brown sugar, cane sugar, and vanilla. Add the dry ingredients to the wet in batches until smooth, then incorporate the shredded carrots, coconut, and walnuts, if using.

3} Using a cookie dropper or tablespoon, drop heaping scoops of dough onto the prepared baking sheets about 2 inches apart. Gently press each cookie down slightly.

4} Bake for 9 to 11 minutes, or until the edges are slightly golden. Remove from the oven and let cool on the baking sheet for 5 minutes, then remove to cool on a wire rack. Let the cookies cool completely. Store in an airtight container.

Ginger Nut Ice Cream
Makes: 1 quart

2 cups nondairy milk (higher fat, like soy or hemp)
¾ cup evaporated cane sugar
1 teaspoon ground ginger
1 teaspoon vanilla extract
1½ cups raw cashews
$\frac{1}{16}$ teaspoon guar gum
⅓ cup finely chopped candied ginger

1} In a large saucepan, whisk together the milk and sugar. Over medium heat, bring the mixture to a boil, whisking frequently. Once it reaches a boil, lower the heat to medium-low and whisk constantly until the sugar is dissolved, about 5 minutes. Remove from the heat, add the ginger and vanilla, and whisk to combine.

2 } Place the cashews in the bottom of a heat-resistant bowl and pour the hot milk mixture over them. Let it cool completely. Once cooled, transfer the mixture to a food processor or high-speed blender and process until smooth, stopping to scrape down the sides as needed. Toward the end of your processing, sprinkle in the guar gum and be sure it is well incorporated.

3 } Pour the mixture into the bowl of a 1½- or 2-quart ice cream maker and process according to the manufacturer's instructions. Once the ice cream is ready, gently mix in the candied ginger. Store in an airtight container in the freezer for at least 2 hours before assembling the sandwiches.

To Make the Sandwiches

1 } Let the ice cream soften slightly so it's easy to scoop. Place half of the cookies, bottoms up, on a clean surface. Scoop one generous scoop of ice cream, about ⅓ cup, onto the top of each cookie. Top the ice cream with the remaining cookies, with the cookie bottoms touching the ice cream. Gently press down on the cookies to level them. Wrap each sandwich in plastic wrap or waxed paper and return to the freezer for at least 30 minutes before serving.

PB & J
Sandwiches

Peanut butter cookies. Peanut butter ice cream with a fruity swirl. 'Nuff said.

Makes: 12 to 16 sandwiches

Peanut Butter Cookies

Makes: about 2 dozen cookies

2 cups unbleached all-purpose flour
2 teaspoons baking soda
¼ teaspoon salt
1 cup nondairy margarine, softened
1 cup evaporated cane sugar
1 cup packed brown sugar
1 teaspoon vanilla extract
1 cup creamy, unsalted natural peanut butter

1 } Preheat the oven to 350°F. Line two baking sheets with parchment paper.

2 } In a small bowl, mix together the flour, baking soda, and salt. In a large bowl, cream together the margarine, cane sugar, brown sugar, and vanilla until creamy. Add the peanut butter and mix well; this may require an electric handheld mixer at a slow speed. In batches, add the dry ingredients to the wet and blend until just mixed.

3} Using a cookie dropper or tablespoon, drop tablespoon-sized scoops of dough onto the prepared baking sheet about 2 inches apart. These cookies spread very nicely, but you can press them with a fork for that classic peanut butter cookie look. Bake for 10 minutes, or until the tops crack and the edges are slightly browned.

4} Remove from the oven and let the cookies cool on the pan for 5 minutes, then transfer to a wire rack. Let the cookies cool completely. Store in an airtight container.

PB & J Soy Ice Cream

Makes: 1¼ quarts

¾ cup evaporated cane sugar
1 tablespoon plus 2 teaspoons tapioca starch
2½ cups soy or hemp milk (full fat)
1 teaspoon coconut oil
2 teaspoons vanilla extract
3 tablespoons creamy, unsalted natural peanut butter
¼ cup good-quality jam or preserves of your choice

1} In a large saucepan, combine the sugar and tapioca starch, and whisk until the starch is incorporated into the sugar. Pour in the milk, whisking to incorporate. Over medium heat, bring the mixture to a boil, whisking frequently. Once it reaches a boil, lower the heat to medium-low and whisk constantly until the mixture thickens and coats the back of a spoon, about 5 minutes. Remove from the heat, add the coconut oil and vanilla, and mix to combine.

2} Transfer the mixture to a heat-resistant bowl and let it cool completely.

3⟩ In small individual bowls, stir the peanut butter and jam until they are smooth. You might need to add a little drizzle of oil (something neutral like vegetable oil) to the peanut butter to make it smooth.

4⟩ Pour the ice cream base into the bowl of a 1½- or 2-quart ice cream maker and process according to the manufacturer's instructions. Once the ice cream is ready, scoop one-third into a freezer-safe container, then add dollops of half of the smooth peanut butter and half of the jam. Add another third of the ice cream and top with the remaining half of the peanut butter and the jam. Top with the last third of the ice cream, then draw a butter knife through the mixture 2 or 3 times to swirl it. Store in an airtight container in the freezer for at least 2 hours before assembling the sandwiches.

To Make the Sandwiches

1⟩ Let the ice cream soften slightly so it's easy to scoop. Place half of the cookies, bottoms up, on a clean surface. Scoop one generous scoop of ice cream, about ⅓ cup, onto the top of each cookie. Top the ice cream with the remaining cookies, with the cookie bottoms touching the ice cream. Gently press down on the cookies to level them out. Wrap each sandwich in plastic wrap or waxed paper and return to the freezer for at least 30 minutes before serving.

Mouthful O' Midwest Sandwiches

Corn and rhubarb are two classic Midwestern summer staples. They grow like weeds and find themselves getting morphed into everything, including ice cream sandwiches.

Yes, you read that right. Sweet corn ice cream. Rhubarb cookies. Suspicious? Cast your doubts aside, put on your overalls, and eat one of these sweet and tangy sandwiches in the summer heat, refreshing yourself after a day in the field, er, lounging on your porch.

Makes: 12 to 16 sandwiches

Rhubarb Cookies

Makes: about 2 dozen cookies

1 ¾ cups unbleached all-purpose flour
1 teaspoon baking powder
¼ teaspoon salt
¾ cup evaporated cane sugar
½ cup nondairy margarine, softened
1 teaspoon vanilla extract
1 cup chopped fresh or frozen (thawed) **rhubarb** (red parts, not green)

1} Preheat the oven to 350°F. Line two baking sheets with parchment paper.

2} In a medium bowl, combine the flour, baking powder, and salt. In a large bowl, cream together the sugar and margarine. Add the vanilla and mix until well combined. Combine the dry ingredients with the wet in batches and mix until smooth. Gently fold in the rhubarb.

3} Using a cookie dropper or tablespoon, drop tablespoon-sized scoops of dough and place on the prepared baking sheets about 1 inch apart. Bake for 9 to 12 minutes, until the cookies have spread and the edges are set and lightly golden.

4} Remove from the oven and let the cookies cool on the pan for 5 minutes, then transfer to a wire rack. Let the cookies cool completely. Store in an airtight container.

Sweet Corn Soy Ice Cream

Makes: 1¼ quarts

2½ cups soy or hemp milk (full fat)
1½ cups sweet corn (fresh preferred, but thawed, frozen corn is fine)
¾ cup evaporated cane sugar
2 teaspoons arrowroot starch
½ teaspoon vanilla extract

1} In the bowl of a food processor or blender, combine the milk and corn and process until smooth. If you're not a fan of texture in your ice cream, pour through a strainer to remove any corn debris (we love that stuff in our house). In a large saucepan, combine the sugar and arrowroot starch, and whisk until the starch is incorporated into the sugar. Pour in the milk/corn mixture, whisking to incorporate. Over medium heat, bring the mixture to a boil, whisking frequently. Once it reaches a boil, lower the heat to medium-low and whisk constantly until the mixture thickens and coats the back of a spoon, about 5 minutes. Remove from the heat, add the vanilla, and whisk to combine.

2} Transfer the mixture to a heat-resistant bowl and let it cool completely.

3} Pour the mixture into the bowl of a 1½- or 2-quart ice cream maker and process according to the manufacturer's instructions. Store in an airtight container in the freezer for at least 2 hours before assembling the sandwiches.

To Make the Sandwiches

1} Let the ice cream soften slightly so it's easy to scoop. Place half of the cookies, bottoms up, on a clean surface. Scoop one generous scoop of ice cream, about ⅓ cup, onto the top of each cookie. Top the ice cream with the remaining cookies, with the cookie bottoms touching the ice cream. Gently press down on the cookies to level them out. Wrap each sandwich in plastic wrap or waxed paper and return to the freezer for at least 30 minutes before serving.

Sandwich Fixin's, Fillin's, and Mixin's

For added fun, make these treats state fair–style: on a stick! After assembling each sandwich, insert a Popsicle stick halfway into the ice cream and wrap the plastic wrap around the stick. Wait at least 3 hours before serving to ensure the stick is stable.

Peanut Butter Bonanza Sandwiches

Vanilla ice cream, studded with chunks of peanut butter cups, smooshed between two chewy, chocolate cookies—whoa. The peanut butter cups take a little advance work, but it's more than worth it.

Makes: 12 to 16 sandwiches

Peanut Butter Cups

Makes: 6 to 8 mini cups

⅓ cup semisweet or dark chocolate chips
¼ cup creamy, salted natural peanut butter (if unsalted, add a pinch of salt)
1 tablespoon powdered sugar

1 } In a small microwave-safe bowl, melt the chocolate in 10-second intervals, stirring between each interval until melted. In a second small bowl combine the peanut butter and powdered sugar.

2 } Line a mini muffin tin with paper liners. Using a silicone brush, paint a solid coat of the melted chocolate over the bottom and sides of the liners. Alternatively, if you have candy molds, you can use those. Chill the chocolate shells in the freezer for 10 to 15 minutes, until solid. Add little scoops of the peanut butter mixture to fill them, then top with a thick layer of chocolate (you may need to reheat the chocolate at this point). This should make 6 to 8 mini peanut butter cups.

3 } Let the peanut butter cups chill in the fridge for 30 minutes or until set. Remove from the paper liners, coarsely chop, and return to the fridge to keep cold.

Chocolate^2 Cookies
Makes: about 2 dozen cookies

1 cup unbleached all-purpose flour
½ cup unsweetened baking cocoa, sifted
½ teaspoon baking soda
¼ teaspoon salt
1 cup evaporated cane sugar
½ cup nondairy margarine, melted and cooled
¼ cup semisweet or dark chocolate chips, melted
1 teaspoon vanilla extract

1 } Preheat the oven to 325°F. Line two baking sheets with parchment paper.

2 } In a medium bowl, combine the flour, cocoa, baking soda, and salt. In a large bowl, cream together the sugar and margarine. Add the melted chocolate and vanilla and mix until well combined. Add the dry ingredients to the wet in batches, and mix until smooth.

3 } Using a cookie dropper or tablespoon, drop heaping scoops of dough onto the prepared baking sheets about 1 inch apart. Bake cookies for 9 to 11 minutes, until the cookies have spread and the edges are set and lightly golden.

4 } Remove from the oven and let the cookies cool on the baking sheets for 5 minutes, then transfer to a cooling rack. Let the cookies cool completely. Store in an airtight container.

Vanilla Peanut Butter Cup Soy Ice Cream

Makes: 1¼ quarts

¾ cup evaporated cane sugar
2 teaspoons arrowroot starch
2½ cups soy or hemp milk (full fat)
½ teaspoon vanilla extract
1 recipe Peanut Butter Cups, chopped

1 } In a large saucepan, combine the sugar and arrowroot starch, and whisk until the starch is incorporated into the sugar. Pour in the milk, whisking to incorporate. Over medium heat, bring the mixture to a boil, whisking frequently. Once it reaches a boil, lower the heat to medium-low, and whisk constantly until the mixture thickens and coats the back of a spoon, about 5 minutes. Remove from the heat add vanilla and whisk to combine.

2 } Transfer the mixture to a heat-resistant bowl and let it cool completely.

3 } Pour the mixture into the bowl of a 1½- or 2-quart ice cream maker and process according to the manufacturer's instructions. Once the ice cream is ready, scoop one-third of it into a freezer-safe container, then add a sprinkle of the chopped peanut butter cups. Add another one-third of the ice cream and top with additional peanut butter cups. Depending on how PB-filled you want it to be, you may or may not want to use all of the peanut butter cups. Your choice. It never hurts to sample a couple (quality

control, you know). Top with the remaining third of the ice cream, then draw a butter knife through the mixture 2 or 3 times, to swirl it. Store in an airtight container in the freezer for at least 2 hours before assembling the sandwiches.

To Make the Sandwiches

1 } Let the ice cream soften slightly so it's easy to scoop. Place half of the cookies, bottoms up, on a clean surface. Scoop one generous scoop of ice cream, about ⅓ cup, onto the top of each cookie. Top the ice cream with the remaining cookies, with the cookie bottoms touching the ice cream. Gently press down on the cookies to level them. Wrap each sandwich in plastic wrap or waxed paper, and return to the freezer for at least 30 minutes before eating.

Sandwich Fixin's, Fillin's, and Mixin's

Make a Frozen Elvis Sandwich by substituting the Banana Cookies on page 38 for the Chocolate Cookies above.

Chai Chowdown
Sandwiches

Chai is a beloved thing. Chai tea. Chai latte. Why not chai ice cream? It's kind of a no-brainer.

Makes: 12 to 16 sandwiches

Crisp Cinnamon Cookies

Makes: about 2 dozen cookies

2 cups unbleached all-purpose flour
1 teaspoon baking powder
1 teaspoon ground cinnamon
¼ teaspoon salt
1 cup plus ¼ cup evaporated cane sugar, divided
½ cup nondairy margarine, melted and cooled to room temperature
½ teaspoon vanilla extract
2 tablespoons nondairy milk, if needed

1 } Preheat the oven to 350°F. Line two baking sheets with parchment paper.

2 } In a small bowl, combine the flour, baking powder, cinnamon, and salt. In a large bowl, cream together 1 cup of the sugar with the melted, cooled margarine and the vanilla. Add the dry ingredients to the wet in batches and mix until smooth. If the dough is not coming together, add a little milk as needed.

3 } Sprinkle the remaining ¼ cup sugar on a small plate. Using a cookie dropper or tablespoon, drop heaping tablespoons of dough onto the prepared baking sheets about 2 inches apart. Using a glass, press the bottom of the glass into the sugar and then press down each cookie with the bottom of the glass until it is about 1½ inches wide. This should apply a scant covering of sugar to the top of each cookie.

4 } Bake for 8 to 10 minutes, or until the edges are slightly golden. Remove from the oven and let cool on the pan for 5 minutes, then remove to cool on a wire rack. Let the cookies cool completely. Store in an airtight container.

Chai Nut Ice Cream

Makes: 1 quart

2 cups soy or hemp milk (full fat)
¾ cup evaporated cane sugar
¼ teaspoon ground cinnamon
¼ teaspoon ground ginger
1 teaspoon vanilla extract
1½ cups raw cashews
4 chai tea bags
¹⁄₁₆ teaspoon guar gum

1 } In a large saucepan, combine the milk and sugar. Over medium heat, bring the mixture to a boil, whisking frequently. Once it reaches a boil, lower the heat to medium-low and whisk constantly until the sugar is dissolved, about 5 minutes. Remove from the heat, add the cinnamon, ginger, and vanilla, and whisk to combine.

2 } Place the cashews and the chai tea bags in the bottom of a heat-resistant bowl and pour the hot milk mixture over them. Let cool completely. Once cooled, squeeze out the tea bags and discard. Transfer the mixture to a food processor or high-speed blender and process until smooth, stopping to scrape down the sides as needed. Toward the end of your processing, sprinkle in the guar gum and be sure it is well incorporated.

3 } Pour the mixture into the bowl of a 1½- or 2-quart ice cream maker and process according to the manufacturer's instructions. Store in an airtight container in the freezer for at least 2 hours before assembling the sandwiches.

To Make the Sandwiches

1 } Let the ice cream soften slightly so it's easy to scoop. Place half of the cookies, bottoms up, on a clean surface. Scoop one generous scoop of ice cream, about ⅓ cup, onto the top of each cookie. Top the ice cream with the remaining cookies, with the cookie bottoms touching the ice cream. Gently press down on the cookies to level them. Wrap each sandwich in plastic wrap or waxed paper and return to the freezer for at least 30 minutes before eating.

Sandwich Fixin's, Fillin's, and Mixin's

Feel free to try with other spiced teas that you like.

Bananas for Chocolate Ice Cream Sandwiches

These sandwiches are beloved by young and old alike. Soft banana cookies and fudge swirled ice cream are always a winning combination.

Makes: 12 to 16 sandwiches

Banana Cookies

Makes: about 2 dozen cookies

1 ¾ cups unbleached all-purpose flour
1 teaspoon baking powder
¼ teaspoon salt
⅔ cup evaporated cane sugar
¼ cup nondairy margarine, softened
1 large roughly mashed, ripe banana (about ½ cup mashed)
1 teaspoon vanilla extract

1} Preheat the oven to 350°F. Line two baking sheets with parchment paper.

2} In a medium bowl, combine the flour, baking powder, and salt. In a large bowl, cream together the sugar and margarine. Add the banana and vanilla, and mix until well combined. Add the dry ingredients to the wet in batches and mix until smooth.

3} Using a cookie dropper or tablespoon, drop tablespoon-sized scoops of dough on the prepared baking sheets about 1 inch apart. Bake for 9 to 12 minutes, until the cookies have spread and the edges are set and lightly golden.

4} Remove from the oven and let the cookies cool on the pan for 5 minutes, then transfer to a wire rack. Let the cookies cool completely. Store in an airtight container.

Fudge Swirl
Makes: ⅓ cup

¼ cup semisweet chocolate chips
1 tablespoon nondairy milk
2 tablespoons nondairy margarine

1} In a microwave-safe bowl, heat the chocolate chips and milk in 15-second increments, stirring between each. Once the chocolate is melted, whisk well to incorporate into the milk. Add the margarine and mix well. Let cool to room temperature.

Vanilla Coconut Ice Cream
Makes: 1 quart

¾ cup evaporated cane sugar
½ teaspoon arrowroot or tapioca starch
1 (13.5-ounce) can full-fat coconut milk (not light)
1 cup nondairy milk
1 teaspoon vanilla extract

1} In a large saucepan, combine the sugar and starch, and whisk until the starch is incorporated into the sugar. Pour in the milk, whisking to incorporate. Over medium heat, bring the mixture to a boil, whisking frequently. Once it reaches a boil, lower the heat to medium-low and whisk constantly until the sugar is dissolved, about 5 minutes. Remove from the heat and add the vanilla, whisking to combine.

2} Transfer the mixture to a heat-resistant bowl and let it cool completely.

3} Pour the mixture into the bowl of a 1½- or 2-quart ice cream maker and process according to the manufacturer's instructions. Once the ice cream is ready, scoop one-third into a freezer-safe container, then add half of the cooled fudge swirl. Add another third of the ice cream and top with the remaining fudge swirl. Top with the last third of the ice cream, then draw a butter knife through the mixture 2 or 3 times, to swirl it. Store in an airtight container in the freezer for at least 2 hours before assembling the sandwiches.

To Make the Sandwiches

1} Let the ice cream soften slightly so it's easy to scoop. Place half of the cookies, bottoms up, on a clean surface. Scoop one generous scoop of ice cream, about ⅓ cup, onto the top of each cookie. Top the ice cream with the remaining cookies, with the cookie bottoms touching the ice cream. Gently press down on the cookies to level them. Wrap each sandwich in plastic wrap or waxed paper and return to the freezer for at least 30 minutes before eating.

Essential Chocolate Chip Ice Cream Sandwiches

It doesn't get more classic Americana than this: chocolate chip cookies and thick vanilla ice cream. Cookie Monster–approved.

Makes: 12 to 16 sandwiches

Chocolate Chip Cookies

Makes: about 2 dozen cookies

2 cups unbleached all-purpose flour
1 teaspoon baking soda
¼ teaspoon salt
½ cup evaporated cane sugar
½ cup packed brown sugar
1 cup nondairy margarine, softened
1 teaspoon cornstarch
2 tablespoons nondairy milk
1 teaspoon vanilla extract
¾ cup semisweet chocolate chips

1} Preheat the oven to 350°F. Line two baking sheets with parchment paper.

2} In a large bowl, sift together the flour, baking soda, and salt. In a second large bowl, cream together the cane sugar, brown sugar, and margarine.

Dissolve the cornstarch in the milk and add to the sugar mixture along with the vanilla. Add the dry ingredients to the wet in batches and mix until combined, then stir in the chocolate chips.

3} Using a cookie dropper or tablespoon, drop heaping scoops of dough onto the prepared baking sheets about 2 inches apart. Bake for 8 to 10 minutes, or until the edges are slightly golden. Remove from the oven and let cool on the pan for 5 minutes, then transfer to a wire rack. Let the cookies cool completely. Store in an airtight container.

Very Vanilla Soy Ice Cream

Makes: 1¼ quarts

¾ cup evaporated cane sugar
2 teaspoons arrowroot or tapioca starch
2½ cups soy or hemp milk (full fat)
1 teaspoon coconut oil
1 vanilla bean, split
½ teaspoon vanilla extract

1} In a large saucepan, combine the sugar and arrowroot or tapioca starch, and whisk until the starch is incorporated into the sugar. Pour in the milk, whisking to incorporate. Over medium heat, bring the mixture to a boil, whisking frequently. Once it reaches a boil, lower the heat to medium-low and whisk constantly until the mixture thickens and coats the back of a spoon, about 5 minutes. Remove from the heat, add the coconut oil, vanilla bean, and vanilla extract, and whisk to combine.

2 } Transfer the mixture to a heat-resistant bowl and let it cool completely. Once cooled, remove the vanilla bean, scraping the seeds into the milk mixture.

3 } Pour the mixture into the bowl of a 1½- or 2-quart ice cream maker and process according to the manufacturer's instructions. Store in an airtight container in the freezer for at least 2 hours before assembling the sandwiches.

To Make the Sandwiches

1 } Let the ice cream soften slightly so it's easy to scoop. Place half of the cookies, bottoms up, on a clean surface. Scoop one generous scoop of ice cream, about ⅓ cup, onto the top of each cookie. Top the ice cream with the remaining cookies, with the cookie bottoms touching the ice cream. Gently press down on the cookies to level them. Wrap each sandwich in plastic wrap or waxed paper and return to the freezer for at least 30 minutes before eating.

Sandwich Fixin's, Fillin's, and Mixin's

Take these sandwiches to a whole new level. Reserve ⅓ cup of the chocolate cookie dough when making the cookies. Chill in the freezer while the ice cream base is cooling. Chop the extra dough into small chunks, and after the ice cream has been processed, gently incorporate the cookie dough chunks, making Chocolate Chip Cookie Dough Chocolate Chip Ice Cream Sandwiches. Wowzers.

Chewy Chocolate
Cookie with Mint
Sandwiches

Chocolate and peppermint are one of those crave-worthy flavor combinations and this sandwich doesn't disappoint.

Makes: 12 to 16 sandwiches

Chewy Chocolate Cookies

Makes: about 2 dozen cookies

⅔ cup nondairy margarine, softened
1 cup evaporated cane sugar
1 teaspoon vanilla extract
1¼ cups unbleached all-purpose flour
½ cup unsweetened baking cocoa, sifted
½ teaspoon baking powder
⅛ teaspoon salt

1} Preheat the oven to 375°F. Line two baking sheets with parchment paper.

2} In a large bowl, cream together the margarine, sugar, and vanilla. In a small bowl, combine the flour, cocoa, baking powder, and salt. Add the dry ingredients to the wet and mix thoroughly.

3} Drop heaping tablespoons of dough onto the prepared baking sheets about 2 inches apart. Bake for 10 to 12 minutes, or until the cookies have spread and the edges are set. Remove from the oven and let cool on the pan for 5 minutes, then transfer to a wire rack. Let the cookies cool completely. Store in an airtight container.

Mint Nut Ice Cream

Makes: 1 quart

2 cups soy or hemp milk (full fat)
¾ cup evaporated cane sugar
1½ teaspoons peppermint extract
1 teaspoon vanilla extract
1½ cups raw cashews
3 to 4 drops green food coloring (optional)
1/16 teaspoon guar gum
⅓ cup semisweet chocolate shavings (use a vegetable peeler on a chocolate bar)

1} In a large saucepan, combine the milk and sugar. Over medium heat, bring the mixture to a boil, whisking frequently. Once it reaches a boil, lower the heat to medium-low and whisk constantly until the sugar is dissolved, about 5 minutes. Remove from the heat and add the peppermint and vanilla extracts, whisking to combine.

2} Place the cashews in the bottom of a heat-resistant bowl and pour the hot milk mixture over them. Let it cool completely. Once cooled, transfer the mixture to a food processor or high-speed blender and process until smooth, stopping to scrape down the sides as needed. Add the food coloring, if using. Toward the end of your processing, sprinkle in the guar gum and be sure it is well incorporated.

3 } Pour the mixture into the bowl of a 1½- or 2-quart ice cream maker and process according to the manufacturer's instructions. Once the ice cream is ready, gently mix in the chocolate shavings. Store in an airtight container in the freezer for at least 2 hours before assembling the sandwiches.

To Make the Sandwiches

1 } Let the ice cream soften slightly so it's easy to scoop. Place half of the cookies, bottoms up, on a clean surface. Scoop one generous scoop of ice cream, about ⅓ cup, onto the top of each cookie. Top the ice cream with the remaining cookies, with the cookie bottoms touching the ice cream. Gently press down on the cookies to level them. Wrap each sandwich in plastic wrap or waxed paper and return to the freezer for at least 30 minutes before eating.

Zucchini Spice
Sandwiches

Is your garden bursting with zucchini? These tasty cookies will provide you with much needed refreshment after hours of tending to your crops.

Makes: 12 to 16 sandwiches

Zucchini Cookies

Makes: about 2 dozen cookies

2 cups unbleached all-purpose flour
½ teaspoon baking powder
1 teaspoon ground cinnamon
¼ teaspoon salt
¾ cup nondairy margarine, at room temperature
¾ cup packed dark brown sugar
½ cup evaporated cane sugar
2 teaspoons vanilla extract
1 cup shredded zucchini
⅓ cup chopped walnuts

1} Preheat the oven to 350°F. Line two baking sheets with parchment paper.

2} In a small bowl, combine the flour, baking powder, cinnamon, and salt. In a large bowl, cream together the margarine, brown sugar, cane sugar, and vanilla. Add the dry ingredients to the wet in batches and mix until smooth, then incorporate the zucchini and walnuts.

3} Using a cookie dropper or tablespoon, drop heaping scoops of dough onto the prepared baking sheet about 2 inches apart. Gently press each cookie down slightly. Bake for 9 to 11 minutes, or until the edges are slightly golden. Remove from the oven and let cool on the pan for 5 minutes, then remove to a wire rack. Let the cookies cool completely. Store in an airtight container.

Spiced Nut Ice Cream

Makes: 1 quart

2 cups soy or hemp milk
¾ cup evaporated cane sugar
1 teaspoon ground cinnamon
½ teaspoon ground ginger
⅛ teaspoon ground allspice
1 teaspoon vanilla extract
1½ cups raw cashews
1/16 teaspoon guar gum

1} In a large saucepan, combine the milk and sugar. Over medium heat, bring the mixture to a boil, whisking frequently. Once it reaches a boil, lower the heat to medium-low and whisk constantly until the sugar is dissolved, about 5 minutes. Remove from the heat and add the cinnamon, ginger, allspice, and vanilla, whisking to combine.

2} Place the cashews in the bottom of a heat-resistant bowl and pour the hot milk mixture over them. Let it cool completely. Once cooled, transfer the mixture to a food processor or high-speed blender and process until smooth, stopping to scrape down the sides as needed. Toward the end of your processing, sprinkle in the guar gum and be sure it is well incorporated.

3 } Pour the mixture into the bowl of a 1½- or 2-quart ice cream maker and process according to the manufacturer's instructions. Store in an airtight container in the freezer for at least 2 hours before assembling the sandwiches.

To Make the Sandwiches

1 } Let the ice cream soften slightly so it's easy to scoop. Place half of the cookies, bottoms up, on a clean surface. Scoop one generous scoop of ice cream, about ⅓ cup, onto the top of each cookie. Top the ice cream with the remaining cookies, with the cookie bottoms touching the ice cream. Gently press down on the cookies to level them. Wrap each sandwich in plastic wrap or waxed paper and return to the freezer for at least 30 minutes before eating.

Sandwich Fixin's, Fillin's, and Mixin's

Shredded apple works equally well in this recipe, if you're plum out of zucchini.

Happy Birthday
Batter Sandwiches

Cake batter ice cream is a novel concept, but with cookies and sprinkles, it's fit for a celebration!

Makes: 12 to 16 sandwiches

Sprinkle Cookies

Makes: about 2 dozen cookies

2 cups unbleached all-purpose flour
1 teaspoon baking soda
¼ teaspoon salt
1 cup packed brown sugar
1 cup nondairy margarine, at room temperature
1 teaspoon cornstarch
2 tablespoons nondairy milk
1½ teaspoons vanilla extract
1½ cups rainbow sprinkles (jimmies) **or other sprinkles of choice, divided**

1} Preheat the oven to 350°F. Line two baking sheets with parchment paper.

2} In a small bowl, combine the flour, baking soda, and salt. In a large bowl, cream together the brown sugar and margarine. Dissolve the cornstarch in the milk and add to the margarine mixture, along with the vanilla. Add the dry ingredients to the wet in batches, stirring until smooth.

3} Using a cookie dropper or tablespoon, drop heaping tablespoons of dough onto the prepared baking sheets about 2 inches apart. Top each cookie with a healthy sprinkle of, um, sprinkles. Bake for 8 to 10 minutes, or until the edges are slightly golden. Remove from the oven and let cool on the pan for 5 minutes, then remove to cool on a wire rack. Let the cookies cool completely. Store in an airtight container.

Cake Batter Soy Ice Cream
Makes: 1¼ quarts

¾ cup evaporated cane sugar
2 teaspoons arrowroot starch
2½ cups soy or hemp milk (full fat)
1¼ teaspoons butter extract (believe it or not, it's vegan!)
1 teaspoon vanilla extract
¼ teaspoon maple extract

1} In a large saucepan, combine the sugar and arrowroot starch, and whisk until the starch is incorporated into the sugar. Pour in the milk, whisking to incorporate. Over medium heat, bring the mixture to a boil, whisking frequently. Once it reaches a boil, lower the heat to medium-low and whisk constantly until the mixture thickens and coats the back of a spoon, about 5 minutes. Remove from the heat, add the butter, vanilla, and maple extracts, and whisk to combine.

2} Transfer the mixture to a heat-resistant bowl and let it cool completely.

3} Pour the mixture into the bowl of a 1½- or 2-quart ice cream maker and process according to the manufacturer's instructions. Store in an airtight container in the freezer for at least an hour before assembling the sandwiches.

To Make the Sandwiches

1} Spread the remaining sprinkles on a small plate. Let the ice cream soften slightly so it's easy to scoop. Place half of the cookies, bottoms up, on a clean surface. Scoop one generous scoop of ice cream, about ⅓ cup, onto the top of each cookie. Top the ice cream with the remaining cookies, with the cookie bottoms touching the ice cream. Gently press down on the cookies to level them. Roll the edges of the ice cream sandwiches in the sprinkles, coating the sides of the ice cream. Wrap each sandwich in plastic wrap or waxed paper and return to the freezer for at least 30 minutes before eating.

Tart Cherry Almond Sandwiches

Amarena is a classic gelato flavor, sweet cream with a tart cherry swirl. This version gets paired up with some vanilla shortbread. Buttery, sweet, and tart, like it's supposed to be.

Makes: 12 to 16 sandwiches

Almond Shortbread Cookies

Makes: about 2 dozen cookies

1 cup nondairy margarine, softened
¾ cup evaporated cane sugar, divided
½ teaspoon almond extract
1 teaspoon vanilla extract
2 cups unbleached all-purpose flour
⅓ cup ground almonds

1} In a large bowl, cream together the margarine, ½ cup of the sugar, and the almond and vanilla extracts until well combined. In a small bowl, combine the flour and ground almonds. Add the flour mixture to the margarine mixture in batches and mix until the dough is soft and smooth. Divide the dough in half and shape each half into a rectangular log, about 5 inches long, 3 inches wide, and 2 inches high. Sprinkle the remaining ¼ cup sugar on a clean surface and roll each log in it, to coat the outside. Wrap each log in plastic wrap and refrigerate for at least 2 hours.

2 } Preheat the oven to 375°F. Line two cookie sheets with parchment paper.

3 } Remove the logs from the fridge and roll each log in the remaining sugar, to coat. Using a sharp knife, cut the logs into ¼-inch-thick slices, pressing the sides of the log as you cut to maintain its shape. Place the sliced cookies on the prepared baking sheets 1 inch apart. Bake for 8 to 10 minutes, or until the edges are lightly browned. If you are baking both sheets at the same time, rotate them halfway through.

4 } Remove from the oven and let the cookies cool on the pan for 5 minutes, then transfer to a wire rack. Let the cookies cool completely. Store in an airtight container.

Tart Cherry Swirl Coconut Ice Cream

Makes: 1 quart

¾ cup plus 2 tablespoons evaporated cane sugar
1 (13.5-ounce) can full-fat coconut milk (not light)
1 cup nondairy milk
1 teaspoon vanilla extract
⅓ cup dried tart cherries, coarsely chopped
¼ cup water
½ teaspoon arrowroot or tapioca starch
½ teaspoon fresh lemon juice

1 } In a large saucepan, combine ¾ cup sugar with the coconut milk and other nondairy milk, whisking to incorporate. Over medium heat, bring the mixture to a boil, whisking frequently. Once it reaches a boil, lower the heat to medium-low and whisk constantly until the sugar is dissolved,

about 5 minutes. Remove from the heat and add the vanilla, whisking to combine.

2 } Transfer the mixture to a heat-resistant bowl and let it cool completely.

3 } While the ice cream base is cooling, combine the dried cherries and water in a small saucepan. Cook over medium heat, until the cherries are softened and the mixture begins to bubble. In a small bowl, combine the remaining 2 tablespoons sugar and the starch. Sprinkle the mixture into the cherries and lower the heat to a simmer. Continue cooking until the mixture thickens, about 3 minutes, then whisk in the lemon juice. Transfer to a heat-resistant bowl to cool completely.

4 } Pour the ice cream base mixture into the bowl of a 1½- or 2-quart ice cream maker and process according to the manufacturer's instructions. Once the ice cream is ready, scoop one-third into a freezer-safe container, then add half of the cooled cherry mixture. Add another third of the ice cream and top with the remaining cherry mixture. Top with the last third of the ice cream, then draw a butter knife through the mixture 2 or 3 times, to swirl it. Store in an airtight container in the freezer for at least 2 hours before assembling the sandwiches.

To Make the Sandwiches

1 } Let the ice cream soften slightly so it is easy to scoop. Place half of the cookies, bottoms up, on a clean surface. Scoop one generous scoop of ice cream, about ⅓ cup, onto the top of each cookie. Top the ice cream with the remaining cookies, with the cookie bottoms touching the ice cream. Gently press down on the cookies to level them. Wrap each sandwich in plastic wrap or waxed paper and return to the freezer for at least 30 minutes before eating.

Oh, Canada
Sandwiches

Thinking of maple syrup when talking about Canada is an American stereotype, but with something so tasty, it's not a *bad* thing, right?

Makes: 12 to 16 sandwiches

Walnut Cookies

Makes: about 2 dozen cookies

2½ cups unbleached all-purpose flour
2 teaspoons baking powder
¼ teaspoon salt
1½ cups evaporated cane sugar
½ cup nondairy margarine, at room temperature
1 teaspoon vanilla extract
2 tablespoons nondairy milk
¾ cup walnuts, coarsely chopped

1 } Preheat the oven to 375°F. Line two baking sheets with parchment paper.

2 } In a medium bowl, combine the flour, baking powder, and salt. In a large bowl, cream together the sugar and margarine. Add the vanilla and milk to the margarine mixture and mix to incorporate. Add the dry ingredients to the wet in batches and mix until smooth. Gently fold in the walnuts.

3 } Using a cookie dropper or tablespoon, drop tablespoon-sized scoops of dough onto the prepared baking sheets about 1 inch apart. Bake for 8 to 10 minutes, until the cookies have spread and the edges are set and lightly golden.

4 } Remove from the oven and let the cookies cool on the pan for 5 minutes, then transfer to a wire rack. Let the cookies cool completely. Store in an airtight container.

Maple Soy Ice Cream

Makes: 1¼ quarts

½ cup evaporated cane sugar
2 teaspoons arrowroot starch
2½ cups soy or hemp milk (full fat)
⅓ cup maple syrup
1 teaspoon maple extract
½ teaspoon vanilla extract

1 } In a large saucepan, combine the sugar and arrowroot starch, and whisk until the starch is incorporated into the sugar. Pour in the milk and maple syrup, whisking to incorporate. Over medium heat, bring the mixture to a boil, whisking frequently. Once it reaches a boil, lower the heat to medium-low and whisk constantly until the mixture thickens and coats the back of a spoon, about 5 minutes. Remove from the heat, add the maple and vanilla extracts, and whisk to combine.

2 } Transfer the mixture to a heat-resistant bowl and let it cool completely.

3 } Pour the mixture into the bowl of a 1½- or 2-quart ice cream maker and process according to the manufacturer's instructions. Store in an airtight container in the freezer for at least 2 hours before assembling the sandwiches.

To Make the Sandwiches

1 } Let the ice cream soften slightly so it's easy to scoop. Place half of the cookies, bottoms up, on a clean surface. Scoop one generous scoop of ice cream, about ⅓ cup, onto the top of each cookie. Top the ice cream with the remaining cookies, with the cookie bottoms touching the ice cream. Gently press down on the cookies to level them. Wrap each sandwich in plastic wrap or waxed paper and return to the freezer for at least 30 minutes before eating.

Coffee Zing
Sandwiches

If you're having one of those days when you want dessert for breakfast, this coffee/chocolate combo is sure to supercharge your morning... or noon or night.

Makes: 12 to 16 sandwiches

Coffee Cookies

Makes: about 2 dozen cookies

2 cups unbleached all-purpose flour
1 teaspoon baking soda
¼ teaspoon salt
1 cup nondairy margarine, at room temperature
½ cup packed brown sugar
½ cup evaporated cane sugar
2 teaspoons instant coffee
2 tablespoons warm nondairy milk
1½ teaspoons vanilla extract

1} Preheat the oven to 350°F. Line two baking sheets with parchment paper.

2} In a small bowl, combine the flour, baking soda, and salt. In a large bowl, cream together the margarine, brown sugar, and cane sugar. Dissolve the instant coffee in the warm milk and add to the margarine mixture along with the vanilla. Add the dry ingredients to the wet in batches until smooth.

3 } Using a cookie dropper or tablespoon, drop heaping tablespoons of dough onto the prepared baking sheets about 2 inches apart. Bake for 8 to 10 minutes, or until the edges are slightly golden. Remove from the oven and let cool on the pan for 5 minutes, then remove to cool on a wire rack. Let the cookies cool completely. Store in an airtight container.

Chocolate Charged Nut Ice Cream

Makes: 1 quart

¾ **cup evaporated cane sugar**
¼ **cup unsweetened baking cocoa, sifted**
2 cups soy or hemp milk (full fat)
1 teaspoon vanilla extract
1½ cups raw cashews
¹⁄₁₆ **teaspoon guar gum**
2 tablespoons chocolate-covered espresso beans, coarsely chopped (optional)

1 } In a large saucepan, combine the sugar and baking cocoa, whisking until there are no lumps. Whisk in the milk. Over medium heat, bring the mixture to a boil, whisking frequently. Once it reaches a boil, lower the heat to medium-low and whisk constantly until the sugar is dissolved, about 5 minutes. Remove from the heat and add the vanilla, whisking to combine.

2 } Place the cashews in the bottom of a heat-resistant bowl and pour the hot milk mixture over them. Let it cool completely. Once cooled, transfer the mixture to a food processor or high-speed blender and process until

smooth, stopping to scrape down the sides as needed. Toward the end of your processing, sprinkle in the guar gum and be sure it is well incorporated.

3 } Pour the mixture into the bowl of a 1½- or 2-quart ice cream maker and process according to the manufacturer's instructions. Once the ice cream is ready, gently mix in the chopped chocolate-covered espresso beans. Store in an airtight container in the freezer for at least 2 hours before assembling the sandwiches.

To Make the Sandwiches

1 } Let the ice cream soften slightly so it's easy to scoop. Place half of the cookies, bottoms up, on a clean surface. Scoop one generous scoop of ice cream, about ⅓ cup, onto the top of each cookie. Top the ice cream with the remaining cookies, with the cookie bottoms touching the ice cream. Gently press down on the cookies to level them. Wrap each sandwich in plastic wrap or waxed paper and return to the freezer for at least 30 minutes before eating.

Tiramisu Sandwiches

Tiramisu in the palm of your hand, on demand! This recipe uses a little tofu in the ice cream, giving it a richer texture, like traditional tiramisu custard.

Makes: 12 to 16 sandwiches

Vanilla Cocoa Cloud Cookies

Makes: about 2 dozen cookies

2½ cups unbleached all-purpose flour
2 teaspoons baking powder
¼ teaspoon salt
1½ cups evaporated cane sugar, divided
½ cup nondairy margarine, at room temperature
½ teaspoon vanilla extract
2 tablespoons nondairy milk
⅓ cup unsweetened baking cocoa, sifted

1} Preheat the oven to 375°F. Line two baking sheets with parchment paper.

2} In a medium bowl, combine the flour, baking powder, and salt. In a large bowl, cream together the sugar and margarine. Add the vanilla and milk, and mix until well combined. Add the dry ingredients to the wet in batches and mix until smooth.

3 } Using a cookie dropper or tablespoon, drop tablespoon-sized scoops of dough onto the prepared baking sheets about 1 inch apart. Bake for 8 to 10 minutes, until the cookies have cracked and spread and the edges are set.

4 } Remove from the oven and immediately sift cocoa powder on the top of the cookies. Let them cool on the pan for 5 minutes, then transfer to a wire rack. Let the cookies cool completely. Store in an airtight container.

Vanilla Soy Custard

Makes: 1¼ quarts

½ cup puréed silken tofu
¾ cup evaporated cane sugar
1 tablespoon arrowroot or tapioca starch
2½ cups soy or hemp milk (full fat), **divided**
1 teaspoon coconut oil
2 teaspoons vanilla extract
2 tablespoons instant espresso powder

1 } Use a food processor to pureé the tofu. In a large saucepan, combine the sugar and starch, and whisk until the starch is incorporated into the sugar. Pour in the tofu purée and 2 cups of the milk, whisking to incorporate. Over medium heat, bring the mixture to a boil, whisking frequently. Once it reaches a boil, lower the heat to medium-low and whisk constantly until the mixture thickens and coats the back of a spoon, about 5 minutes. Remove from the heat, add the coconut oil and vanilla, and mix to combine.

2 } Transfer the mixture to a heat-resistant bowl and let it cool completely.

3 } Pour the mixture into the bowl of a 1½- or 2-quart ice cream maker and process according to the manufacturer's instructions. Store in an airtight container in the freezer for at least 2 hours before assembling the sandwiches.

4 } Heat the remaining ½ cup of milk in the microwave until just warm. Whisk in the instant espresso and mix until dissolved. Let it cool to room temperature.

To Make the Sandwiches

1 } Let the ice cream soften slightly so it's easy to scoop. Place half of the cookies, bottoms up, on a clean surface. Scoop one generous scoop of ice cream, about ⅓ cup, onto the top of each cookie. Dip the bottom of each of the top cookies into the espresso and give it just a moment to absorb slightly. Top the ice cream with the espresso-soaked cookies, with the cookie bottoms touching the ice cream. Gently press down on the cookies to level them. Wrap each sandwich in plastic wrap or waxed paper and return to the freezer for at least 30 minutes before eating.

Lemon Raspberry
Pucker Sandwiches

Tart lemon and creamy raspberry sherbet make a tangy and refreshing combination.

Makes: 12 to 16 sandwiches

Lemon Cornmeal Cookies

Makes: about 2 dozen cookies

1½ cups unbleached all-purpose flour
½ cup finely ground yellow cornmeal
2 teaspoons cornstarch
½ teaspoon salt
¾ cup evaporated cane sugar
¾ cup nondairy margarine, softened
grated zest of 1 lemon
2 tablespoons fresh lemon juice
1 teaspoon vanilla extract

1 } Preheat the oven to 350°F. Prepare two baking sheets with parchment paper.

2 } In a medium bowl, combine the flour, cornmeal, cornstarch, and salt. In a large bowl, cream together the sugar and margarine. Add the lemon zest, lemon juice, and vanilla to the margarine mixture and stir to incorporate. Add the dry ingredients to the wet in batches and mix until smooth.

3 } Using a cookie dropper or tablespoon, drop heaping tablespoons of dough onto the prepared baking sheets about 1 inch apart. Flatten each one slightly. Bake for 11 to 13 minutes, until the cookies have spread and the edges are set and lightly golden.

4 } Remove from the oven and let cool on the sheet for 5 minutes, then transfer to a wire rack. Let the cookies cool completely. Store in an airtight container.

Raspberry Sherbet

Makes: 1 quart

2½ cups fresh or frozen raspberries
2 cups soy or hemp milk, or low-fat coconut milk
¾ cup evaporated cane sugar
1 teaspoon fresh lemon juice

1 } In a food processor or high-speed blender, purée the raspberries until smooth. If you don't like seeds, strain the mixture through a fine-mesh sieve into a bowl. Set the purée aside.

2 } In a large saucepan, combine the milk and sugar, whisking to combine. Over medium heat, bring the mixture to a boil, whisking frequently. Once it reaches a boil, add the raspberry purée and lower the heat to a simmer, stirring often, until the sugar is dissolved, about 5 minutes. Remove from the heat, add the lemon juice, and whisk to combine.

3 } Transfer the mixture to a heat-resistant bowl and let it cool completely.

4} Pour the mixture into the bowl of a 1½- or 2-quart ice cream maker and process according to the manufacturer's instructions. Store in an airtight container in the freezer for at least 2 hours before assembling the sandwiches.

To Make the Sandwiches

1} Let the sherbet soften slightly so it's easy to scoop. Place half of the cookies, bottoms up, on a clean surface. Scoop one generous scoop of sherbet, about ⅓ cup, onto the top of each cookie. Top with the remaining cookies, with the cookie bottoms touching the sherbet. Gently press down on the cookies to level them. Wrap each sandwich in plastic wrap or waxed paper, and return to the freezer for at least 30 minutes before eating.

Sandwich Fixin's, Fillin's, and Mixin's

Substitute lime for the lemon in the cookies and cherries for the raspberries in the ice cream for a different take on this combination.

Orange Dreamsicle
Sandwiches

Crisp vanilla cookies and creamy orange ice cream are the things dreams are made of.

Makes: 12 to 16 sandwiches

Crisp Vanilla Cookies

Makes: about 2 dozen cookies

2½ cups unbleached all-purpose flour
1 teaspoon baking powder
¼ teaspoon salt
1 cup plus ¼ cup evaporated cane sugar, divided
½ cup nondairy margarine, melted and cooled to room temperature
½ teaspoon vanilla extract
2 tablespoons nondairy milk, if needed

1} Preheat the oven to 350°F. Line two baking sheets with parchment paper.

2} In a small bowl, combine the flour, baking powder, and salt. In a large bowl, cream 1 cup of the sugar together with the melted margarine and vanilla. Add the dry ingredients to the wet in batches until smooth. If the dough is not coming together, add a little milk as needed.

3} Sprinkle the remaining ¼ cup sugar on a small plate. Using a cookie dropper or tablespoon, drop heaping tablespoons of dough about 2 inches apart. Using a glass, press the bottom of the glass into the sugar and then press down each cookie with the bottom of the glass until it is about 1½ inches wide. This should apply a scant covering of sugar to the top of each cookie.

4} Bake for 8 to 10 minutes, or until the edges are slightly golden. Remove from the oven and let cool on the pan for 5 minutes, then remove to cool on a wire rack. Let the cookies cool completely. Store in an airtight container.

Orange Coconut Cream Ice Cream

Makes: 1 quart

1 (13.5-ounce) can full-fat coconut milk (not light)
⅔ cup nondairy milk
⅓ cup fresh orange juice
¾ cup evaporated cane sugar
2 teaspoons grated orange zest
1 teaspoon vanilla extract

1} In a large saucepan, combine the coconut and nondairy milk. Add the orange juice and sugar and whisk to combine. Over medium heat, bring the mixture to a boil, whisking frequently. Once it reaches a boil, lower the heat to medium-low and whisk constantly until the sugar is dissolved, about 5 minutes. Remove from the heat and add the grated orange zest and vanilla, whisking to combine.

2} Transfer the mixture to a heat-resistant bowl and let it cool completely.

3 } Pour the mixture into the bowl of a 1½- or 2-quart ice cream maker and process according to the manufacturer's instructions. Store in an airtight container in the freezer for at least 2 hours before assembling the sandwiches.

To Make the Sandwiches

1 } Let the ice cream soften slightly so it's easy to scoop. Place half of the cookies, bottoms up, on a clean surface. Scoop one generous scoop of ice cream, about ⅓ cup, onto the top of each cookie. Top the ice cream with the remaining cookies, with the cookie bottoms touching the ice cream. Gently press down on the cookies to level them. Wrap each sandwich in plastic wrap or waxed paper and return to the freezer for at least 30 minutes before eating.

Root Beer Float
Sandwiches

In a parallel world, root beer floats fit into the palm of your hand, a solid treat where the root beer is cold and creamy...wait, that's not a different world. It's here and now!

Makes: 12 to 16 sandwiches

Very Vanilla Cookies

Makes: about 2 dozen cookies

2½ cups unbleached all-purpose flour
2 teaspoons baking powder
¼ teaspoon salt
1½ cups evaporated cane sugar
½ cup nondairy margarine, at room temperature
1 teaspoon vanilla extract
1 vanilla bean, split open and seeds scraped out
2 tablespoons nondairy milk

1} Preheat the oven to 375°F. Line two baking sheets with parchment paper.

2} In a medium bowl, combine the flour, baking powder, and salt. In a large bowl, cream together the sugar and margarine. In a small bowl, add the vanilla extract and seeds to the milk and mix until well combined. Add the vanilla mixture to the margarine mixture and incorporate. Add the dry ingredients to the wet in batches and mix until smooth.

3} Using a cookie dropper or tablespoon, drop tablespoon-sized scoops of dough onto the prepared baking sheets about 1 inch apart. Bake for 8 to 10 minutes, until the cookies have spread and the edges are set and lightly golden.

4} Remove from the oven and let the cookies cool on the pan for 5 minutes, then transfer to a wire rack. Let the cookies cool completely. Store in an airtight container.

Root Beer Coconut Ice Cream

Makes: 1 quart

1 (13.5-ounce) can full-fat coconut milk (not light)
1 cup nondairy milk
¾ cup evaporated cane sugar
2 teaspoons root beer concentrate
1 teaspoon vanilla extract

1} In a large saucepan, combine the coconut and nondairy milk. Add the sugar and whisk to combine. Over medium heat, bring the mixture to a boil, whisking frequently. Once it reaches a boil, lower the heat to medium-low and whisk constantly until the sugar is dissolved, about 5 minutes. Remove from the heat and add the root beer concentrate and vanilla, whisking to combine.

2} Transfer the mixture to a heat-resistant bowl and let it cool completely. Once it's cooled, check to see if it's root beer-y enough for you. Keep in mind that the flavor will intensify as it sits. Add more concentrate if you're a risk taker.

3 } Pour the mixture into the bowl of a 1½- or 2-quart ice cream maker and process according to the manufacturer's instructions. Store in an airtight container in the freezer for at least 2 hours before assembling the sandwiches.

To Make the Sandwiches

1 } Let the ice cream soften slightly so it's easy to scoop. Place half of the cookies, bottoms up, on a clean surface. Scoop one generous scoop of ice cream, about ⅓ cup, onto the top of each cookie. Top the ice cream with the remaining cookies, with the cookie bottoms touching the ice cream. Gently press down on the cookies to level them. Wrap each sandwich in plastic wrap or waxed paper and return to the freezer for at least 30 minutes before eating.

Holiday Cranberry
Snap Sandwiches

I briefly lived in the Southwest and Christmas never quite felt like Christmas down there, although I imagine these sandwiches would have helped. I'm a Midwesterner again, but these certainly don't hurt the holiday spirit.

Makes: 12 to 16 sandwiches

Gingersnaps

Makes: about 2 dozen cookies

2 cups unbleached all-purpose flour
½ teaspoon baking soda
1 teaspoon ground ginger
1 teaspoon ground cinnamon
¼ teaspoon freshly ground nutmeg
¼ teaspoon salt
½ cup plus 3 tablespoons evaporated cane sugar, divided
½ cup packed brown sugar
¾ cup nondairy margarine, softened
2 tablespoons molasses
1 tablespoon nondairy milk
½ teaspoon vanilla extract

1} Preheat the oven to 350°F. Line two baking sheets with parchment paper.

2 } In a medium bowl, combine the flour, baking soda, ginger, cinnamon, nutmeg, and salt. In a large bowl, cream together ½ cup of the cane sugar with the brown sugar and margarine. Add the molasses, milk, and vanilla and stir to incorporate. Add the dry ingredients to the wet in batches and mix until smooth.

3 } Sprinkle the remaining 3 tablespoons of sugar on a small plate. Using a cookie dropper or tablespoon, scoop out tablespoon-sized dough balls and roll in the sugar to coat, then place on the prepared baking sheets about 1 inch apart. Flatten each one slightly. Bake for 11 to 13 minutes, until the cookies have spread and the edges are set.

4 } Remove from the oven and let the cookies cool on the pan for 5 minutes, then transfer to a wire rack. Let the cookies cool completely. Store in an airtight container.

Cranberry Ice Cream

Makes: 1 quart

2 cups fresh cranberries
1 cup evaporated cane sugar
⅔ cup water
2 teaspoons arrowroot or tapioca starch
2 cups soy or hemp milk
½ teaspoon vanilla extract

1 } In a large saucepan, combine the cranberries, sugar, and water, and stir to combine. Over medium heat, cook until the mixture begins to bubble, whisking frequently. Once it starts bubbling, the cranberries will begin to

split; lower the heat to low and give them a hand using a potato masher or the back of a strong fork. Whisk constantly until the mixture thickens, 3 to 5 minutes, then remove from the heat. If you would like, put the mixture through a strainer or skim the top to remove the skins. Sprinkle the starch over the mixture and stir to combine.

2 } Return the saucepan to the stove and whisk in the milk. Whisking constantly, cook over medium heat until the mixture thickens and coats the back of a spoon, about 5 minutes. Remove from the heat, add the vanilla, and whisk to combine.

3 } Transfer the mixture to a heat-resistant bowl and let it cool completely.

4 } Pour the mixture into the bowl of a 1½- or 2-quart ice cream maker and process according to the manufacturer's instructions. Store in an airtight container in the freezer for at least 2 hours before assembling the sandwiches.

To Make the Sandwiches

1 } Let the ice cream soften slightly so it is easy to scoop. Place half of the cookies, bottoms up, on a clean surface. Scoop one generous scoop of ice cream, about ⅓ cup, onto the top of each cookie. Top the ice cream with the remaining cookies, with the cookie bottoms touching the ice cream. Gently press down on the cookies to level them. Wrap each sandwich in plastic wrap or waxed paper and return to the freezer for at least 30 minutes before eating.

Shirley Temple Sandwiches

Drinking's never been my thing, so I've had a lifetime relationship with the Shirley Temple. Forgo the red dye #40 and take it to the next level with these tart and chewy sandwiches.

Makes: 12 to 16 sandwiches

Chewy Cherry Cookies

Makes: about 2 dozen cookies

1 cup unbleached all-purpose flour
½ teaspoon baking soda
⅛ teaspoon salt
½ cup evaporated cane sugar
½ cup packed brown sugar
½ cup plus 2 tablespoons nondairy margarine, melted and cooled
1 teaspoon vanilla extract
1 cup quick-cooking or old-fashioned oats
⅔ cup dried cherries

1 } Preheat the oven to 350°F. Line two baking sheets with parchment paper.

2 } In a medium bowl, combine the flour, baking soda, and salt. In a large bowl, cream the cane sugar together with the brown sugar and margarine. Add the vanilla to the margarine mixture and incorporate. Add the dry

ingredients to the wet in batches and mix until just smooth. Gently fold in the oats and cherries until mixed.

3} Using a cookie dropper or tablespoon, drop tablespoon-sized scoops of dough onto the prepared baking sheets about 1 inch apart. Flatten each cookie slightly. Bake for 11 to 13 minutes, until the cookies have spread and the edges are set.

4} Remove from the oven and let the cookies cool on the pan for 5 minutes, then transfer to a wire rack. Let the cookies cool completely. Store in an airtight container.

Lemon-Lime Sherbet

Makes: 1 quart

1 cup fresh lemon juice
½ cup fresh lime juice
⅔ cup evaporated cane sugar
¾ cup soy, hemp, coconut, or nut milk
grated zest of 1 lemon
grated zest of 1 lime

1} In a large saucepan, combine the lemon juice, lime juice, and sugar. Whisk together and cook over medium-high heat until bubbling, about 4 minutes. Lower the heat to medium-low and continue to cook until the sugar has dissolved. Remove from the heat and whisk in the milk and lemon and lime zests.

2} Transfer the mixture to a heat-resistant bowl and let it cool completely.

3 } Pour the mixture into the bowl of a 1½- or 2-quart ice cream maker and process according to the manufacturer's instructions. Store in an airtight container in the freezer for at least 2 hours before assembling the sandwiches.

To Make the Sandwiches

1 } Let the sherbet soften slightly, so it is easy to scoop. Place half of the cookies, bottoms up, on a clean surface. Scoop one generous scoop of sherbet, about ⅓ cup, onto the top of each cookie. Top the sherbet with the remaining cookies, with the cookie bottoms touching the sherbet. Gently press down on the cookies to level them. Wrap each sandwich in plastic wrap or waxed paper and return to the freezer for at least 30 minutes before eating.

Pistachio Cardamom Dream Sandwiches

I have a special place in my heart for pistachio, well, anything! The pistachio lover in your life will bow before you with gratitude for these sandwiches.

Makes: 12 to 16 sandwiches

Cardamom Cookies

Makes: about 2 dozen cookies

2 cups unbleached all-purpose flour
1 teaspoon baking powder
1½ teaspoons ground cardamom
¼ teaspoon salt
1 cup evaporated cane sugar
½ cup nondairy margarine, melted and cooled to room temperature
½ teaspoon vanilla extract
2 tablespoons nondairy milk, if needed

1} Preheat the oven to 350°F. Line two baking sheets with parchment paper.

2} In a small bowl, combine the flour, baking powder, cardamom, and salt. In a large bowl, cream the sugar together with the melted margarine and vanilla. Add the dry ingredients to the wet in batches and mix until smooth. If the dough is not coming together, add a little milk as needed.

3 } Using a cookie dropper or tablespoon, drop tablespoon-sized scoops of dough onto the prepared baking sheets about 2 inches apart. Press the dough down slightly. Bake for 8 to 10 minutes, until the cookies have spread and the edges are set and lightly golden.

4 } Remove from the oven and let cool on the pan for 5 minutes, then remove to a wire rack. Let the cookies cool completely. Store in an airtight container.

Pistachio Nut Ice Cream

Makes: 1 quart

2 cups soy or hemp milk (full fat)
¾ cup evaporated cane sugar
1 teaspoon vanilla extract
1 cup shelled unsalted pistachios
¹⁄₁₆ teaspoon guar gum

1 } In a large saucepan, combine the milk and sugar. Over medium heat, bring the mixture to a boil, whisking frequently. Once it reaches a boil, lower the heat and whisk constantly until the sugar is dissolved, about 5 minutes. Remove from the heat and add the vanilla, whisking to combine.

2 } Place the pistachios in the bottom of a heat-resistant bowl and pour the hot milk mixture over them. Let it cool completely. Once cooled, transfer the mixture to a food processor or high-speed blender and process until smooth, stopping to scrape down the sides as needed. Toward the end of your processing, sprinkle in the guar gum and be sure it is well incorporated.

3 } Pour the mixture into the bowl of a 1½- or 2-quart ice cream maker and process according to the manufacturer's instructions. Store in an airtight container in the freezer for at least 2 hours before assembling the sandwiches.

To Make the Sandwiches

1 } Let the ice cream soften slightly so it's easy to scoop. Place half of the cookies, bottoms up, on a clean surface. Scoop one generous scoop of ice cream, about ⅓ cup, onto the top of each cookie. Top the ice cream with the remaining cookies, with the cookie bottoms touching the ice cream. Gently press down the cookies to level them. Wrap each sandwich in plastic wrap or waxed paper and return to the freezer for at least 30 minutes before eating.

Shimmy Mango Coconut Sandwiches

Mango and coconut play so well off each other, these sandwiches are sure to bring a little bit of the tropics to wherever you are.

Makes: 12 to 16 sandwiches

Coconut Cookies

Makes: about 2 dozen cookies

2 cups unbleached all-purpose flour
¾ cup unsweetened shredded coconut
2 teaspoons baking powder
¼ teaspoon salt
1¼ cups evaporated cane sugar, divided
¼ cup coconut oil, melted and slightly cooled
¼ cup nondairy margarine, at room temperature
½ teaspoon vanilla extract
2 tablespoons nondairy milk

1} Preheat the oven to 375°F. Line two baking sheets with parchment paper.

2} In a medium bowl, combine the flour, shredded coconut, baking powder, and salt. In a large bowl, cream together the sugar, coconut oil, and margarine. Add the vanilla and milk, and mix until well combined. Add the dry ingredients to the wet in batches and mix until smooth.

3} Using a cookie dropper or tablespoon, drop heaping tablespoons of dough onto the prepared baking sheets about 1 inch apart. Bake for 9 to 11 minutes, until the cookies have cracked and spread and the edges are lightly golden.

4} Remove from the oven and let the cookies cool on the sheet for 5 minutes, then transfer to a wire rack. Let the cookies cool completely. Store in an airtight container.

Mango Sorbet

Makes: 1 quart

½ cup evaporated cane sugar
¾ cup water
1 tablespoon coconut oil
2 to 3 large, ripe mangoes or frozen mango chunks, equal to 3 cups chopped

1} In a small saucepan, combine the sugar and water, and bring the mixture to a boil, whisking frequently. Lower the heat to a simmer and whisk, cooking until the sugar is dissolved, about 2 minutes. Remove from the heat, add the coconut oil, and whisk to combine.

2} Pour the sugar mixture and mango into a high-speed blender or food processor and blend until smooth, scraping down the sides as needed.

3} Transfer the mixture to a heat-resistant bowl and let it cool completely.

4 } Pour the mixture into the bowl of a 1½- or 2-quart ice cream maker and process according to the manufacturer's instructions. Store in an airtight container in the freezer for at least 2 hours before assembling the sandwiches.

To Make the Sandwiches

1 } Let the sorbet soften slightly so it's easy to scoop. Place half of the cookies, bottoms up, on a clean surface. Scoop one generous scoop of sorbet, about ⅓ cup, onto the top of each cookie. Top the sorbet with the remaining cookies, with the cookie bottoms touching the ice cream. Gently press down on the cookies to level them. If desired, press a little toasted, shredded coconut into the side of the sorbet for garnish. Wrap each sandwich in plastic wrap or waxed paper, and return to the freezer for at least 30 minutes before serving.

Sandwich Fixin's, Fillin's, and Mixin's

Swapping out the mango for pineapple is never a bad idea...

Chocolate Cookie
Crunch Sandwiches

When you put a cookie...inside of a cookie...what does it mean? Don't go too far down the philosophical rabbit hole without one of these sandwiches to fuel you. Crushed chocolate sandwich cookies stirred into sweet and creamy ice cream, sandwiched between chocolate cookies and frozen. It's chock-full of tastiness.

Makes: 12 to 16 sandwiches

Chocolate Shortbread Cookies

Makes: about 2 dozen cookies

1 cup nondairy margarine, softened
½ cup evaporated cane sugar, divided
1½ teaspoons vanilla extract
1¾ cups unbleached all-purpose flour
½ cup unsweetened baking cocoa, sifted

1} In a large bowl, cream together the margarine, sugar, and vanilla until well combined. In a small bowl, combine the flour and cocoa. Add the dry ingredients to the wet and mix until the dough is soft and smooth. Divide the dough in half and shape each half into a rectangular log, about 5 inches long, 3 inches high, and 2 inches wide. Wrap each log in plastic wrap and refrigerate for at least 2 hours.

2} Preheat the oven to 375°F. Line two baking sheets with parchment paper.

3 } Remove the logs from the fridge. Using a sharp knife, cut the logs into ¼-inch-thick slices, pressing the sides of the log as you cut to maintain its shape. Place the sliced cookies on the prepared baking sheets 1 inch apart. Bake for 8 to 10 minutes, until the edges are set.

4 } Remove from the oven and let the cookies cool on the pan for 5 minutes, then transfer to a wire rack. Let the cookies cool completely. Store in an airtight container.

Cookie Crunch Soy Ice Cream

Makes: 1¼ quarts

¾ cup evaporated cane sugar
1 tablespoon plus 2 teaspoons tapioca starch
2½ cups soy or hemp milk (full fat)
1 teaspoon coconut oil
2 teaspoons vanilla extract
6 to 8 chocolate sandwich cookies, crushed

1 } In a large saucepan, combine the sugar and tapioca starch, and whisk until the starch is incorporated into the sugar. Pour in the milk, whisking to incorporate. Over medium heat, bring the mixture to a boil, whisking frequently. Once it reaches a boil, lower the heat to medium-low and whisk constantly until the mixture thickens and coats the back of a spoon, about 5 minutes. Remove from the heat, add the coconut oil and vanilla, and mix to combine.

2 } Transfer the mixture to a heat-resistant bowl and let it cool completely.

3 } Pour the mixture into the bowl of a 1½- or 2-quart ice cream maker and process according to the manufacturer's instructions. Once set, gently mix in the cookie crumbles using a spatula. Store in an airtight container in the freezer for at least 2 hours before assembling the sandwiches.

To Make the Sandwiches

1 } Let the ice cream soften slightly so it's easy to scoop. Place half of the cookies, bottoms up, on a clean surface. Scoop one generous scoop of ice cream, about ⅓ cup, onto the top of each cookie. Top the ice cream with the remaining cookies, with the cookie bottoms touching the ice cream. Gently press down on the cookies to level them. Wrap each sandwich in plastic wrap or waxed paper and return to the freezer for at least 30 minutes before eating.

Banana Split
Sandwiches

You know you're having a good day when you can double-fist banana splits. These sandwiches make it possible and much less messy than the traditional version.

Makes: 12 to 16 sandwiches

Peanut Chunk Cookies

Makes: about 2 dozen cookies

2½ cups unbleached all-purpose flour
2 teaspoons baking powder
¼ teaspoon salt
1½ cups evaporated cane sugar
½ cup nondairy margarine, at room temperature
1 teaspoon vanilla extract
¼ cup creamy natural peanut butter
¾ cup candied peanuts, coarsely chopped

1} Preheat the oven to 375°F. Prepare two baking sheets with parchment paper.

2} In a medium bowl, combine the flour, baking powder, and salt. In a large bowl, cream together the sugar and margarine. Add the vanilla and peanut butter to the margarine mixture and incorporate; this may require an electric handheld mixer at a slow speed. Add the dry ingredients to the wet in batches and mix until smooth. Gently fold in the peanuts.

3} Using a cookie dropper or tablespoon, drop tablespoon-sized scoops of dough onto the prepared baking sheets about 1 inch apart. Bake for 8 to 10 minutes, until the cookies have spread and the edges are set and lightly golden.

4} Remove from the oven and let the cookies cool on the pan for 5 minutes, then transfer to a wire rack. Let the cookies cool completely. Store in an airtight container.

Banana Split Coconut Ice Cream

Makes: 1 quart

¾ cup evaporated cane sugar
1 (13.5-ounce) can full-fat coconut milk (not light)
1 cup nondairy milk
1 teaspoon vanilla extract
1 large, ripe banana, chopped
⅓ cup fresh or frozen and thawed strawberries, chopped
⅓ cup fresh or frozen and thawed pineapple chunks, chopped

1} In a large saucepan, combine the sugar, coconut milk, and nondairy milk, whisking to incorporate. Over medium heat, bring the mixture to a boil, whisking frequently. Once it reaches a boil, lower the heat to medium-low and whisk constantly until the sugar is dissolved, about 5 minutes. Remove from the heat and add the vanilla, whisking to combine.

2} Transfer the mixture to a heat-resistant bowl and let it cool completely.

3 } Pour the mixture into the bowl of a 1½- or 2-quart ice cream maker and process according to the manufacturer's instructions. Once the ice cream is set, stir in the banana, strawberry, and pineapple chunks with a spatula to combine. Store in an airtight container in the freezer for at least 2 hours before assembling the sandwiches.

Chocolate Schmear

Makes: ⅔ cup

½ cup semisweet chocolate chips
2 tablespoons nondairy milk
3 tablespoons nondairy margarine

1 } In a microwave-safe bowl, melt the chocolate chips and milk in 15-second increments, stirring between each. Once melted, whisk well to incorporate. Add the margarine and whisk well. Let cool to room temperature.

To Make the Sandwiches

1 } Let the ice cream soften slightly so it is easy to scoop. Place half of the cookies, bottoms up, on a clean surface. Scoop one generous scoop of ice cream, about ⅓ cup, onto the top of each cookie. Spread a hearty tablespoon of chocolate schmear onto the bottoms of the remaining cookies, then top the ice cream with the schmeared cookie. Gently press down on the cookies to even them out. Wrap each sandwich in plastic wrap or waxed paper and return to the freezer for at least 30 minutes before eating.

Peach Rum Crumble
Sandwiches

A baking staple, the humble crumble is given a new spin in this creamy, sweet delight, with a little oatmeal crunch for good measure.

Makes: 12 to 16 sandwiches

Oat Crumble Cookies

Makes: about 2 dozen cookies

1 cup unbleached all-purpose flour
½ teaspoon baking soda
⅛ teaspoon salt
½ cup evaporated cane sugar
½ cup packed brown sugar
½ cup plus 2 tablespoons nondairy margarine, melted and cooled
1 teaspoon vanilla extract
1 cup quick-cooking or old-fashioned oats

1} Preheat the oven to 350°F. Line two baking sheets with parchment paper.

2} In a medium bowl, combine the flour, baking soda, and salt. In a large bowl, cream the cane sugar together with the brown sugar and margarine. Add the vanilla to the margarine mixture and incorporate. Add the dry ingredients to the wet in batches and mix until just smooth. Gently fold in the oats until mixed.

3 } Using a cookie dropper or tablespoon, drop tablespoon-sized scoops of dough onto the prepared baking sheets about 1 inch apart. Bake for 11 to 13 minutes, until the cookies have spread and the edges are set.

4 } After removing from the oven, let the cookies cool on the pan for 5 minutes, then transfer to a wire rack. Let the cookies cool completely. Store in an airtight container.

Pecan & Peaches Ice Cream
Makes: 1¼ quarts

2 cups soy or hemp milk (full fat)
¾ cup evaporated cane sugar
1 teaspoon vanilla extract
1½ teaspoons rum extract (optional)
¾ cup raw cashews
¾ cup toasted pecans
1/16 teaspoon guar gum
¾ cup coarsely chopped peaches, fresh or frozen and thawed

1 } In a large saucepan, combine the milk and sugar. Over medium heat, bring the mixture to a boil, whisking frequently. Once it reaches a boil, lower the heat to medium-low and whisk constantly until the sugar is dissolved, about 5 minutes. Remove from the heat and add the vanilla and rum extracts, if using rum, whisking to combine.

2 } Place the cashews and pecans in the bottom of a heat-resistant bowl and pour the hot milk mixture over them. Let it cool completely. Once cooled, transfer the mixture to a food processor or high-speed blender and process until smooth, stopping to scrape down the sides as needed.

Toward the end of your processing, sprinkle in the guar gum and be sure it is well incorporated.

3 } Pour the mixture into the bowl of a 1½- or 2-quart ice cream maker and process according to the manufacturer's instructions. Once the ice cream is ready, gently mix in the peach chunks. Store in an airtight container in the freezer for at least 2 hours before assembling the sandwiches.

To Make the Sandwiches

1 } Let the ice cream soften slightly so it is easy to scoop. Place half of the cookies, bottoms up, on a clean surface. Scoop one generous scoop of ice cream onto the top of each cookie, about ⅓ cup. Top the ice cream with the remaining cookies, with the cookie bottoms touching the ice cream. Gently press down on the cookies to level them. Wrap each sandwich in plastic wrap or waxed paper and return to the freezer for at least 30 minutes before serving.

Early Grey with Orange Sandwiches

Ice cream infused with Earl Grey tea and crisp, zesty orange cookies are a pairing perfect for tea (or any other) time.

Makes: 12 to 16 sandwiches

Orange Zest Shortbread Cookies

Makes: about 2 dozen cookies

1 cup nondairy margarine, softened
½ cup evaporated cane sugar
grated zest of 1 orange
2 tablespoons fresh orange juice
1 teaspoon vanilla extract
2¼ cups unbleached all-purpose flour

1} In a large bowl, cream together the margarine, sugar, orange zest, orange juice, and vanilla until well combined. Add the flour to the margarine mixture in batches and mix until the dough is soft and smooth. Divide the dough in half and shape each half into a rectangular log, about 5 inches long, 3 inches high, and 2 inches wide. Wrap each log in plastic wrap and refrigerate for at least 2 hours.

2} Preheat the oven to 375°F. Line two baking sheets with parchment paper.

3 } Remove the logs from the fridge. Using a sharp knife, cut the logs into ¼-inch-thick slices, pressing the sides of the log as you cut to maintain its shape. Place the sliced cookies on the prepared baking sheets 1 inch apart. Bake for 8 to 10 minutes or until the edges are lightly browned.

4 } Remove from the oven and let the cookies cool on the pan for 5 minutes, then transfer to a wire rack. Let the cookies cool completely. Store in an airtight container.

Early Grey Soy Ice Cream

Makes: 1¼ quarts

¾ cup evaporated cane sugar, divided
2½ cups soy or hemp milk (full fat)
6 Earl Grey tea bags
1 tablespoon plus 2 teaspoons arrowroot or tapioca starch
2 teaspoons vanilla extract

1 } In a large saucepan, combine ½ cup of the sugar and the milk, whisking to incorporate. Over medium heat, bring the mixture to a boil, whisking frequently. Once it reaches a boil, remove from the heat, place the tea bags in the pan, and steep, covered, for 15 minutes. While the tea is steeping, combine the remaining sugar and starch in a small bowl. Remove the tea bags (carefully squeezing them out), and return the pan to medium heat and whisk in the sugar/starch mixture. Bring the mixture to a boil and then reduce the heat to low. Whisk constantly until the mixture thickens and coats the back of a spoon, about 5 minutes. Remove from the heat, add the vanilla, and mix to combine.

Vegan Ice Cream **Sandwiches**

2 } Transfer the mixture to a heat-resistant bowl and let it cool completely.

3 } Pour the mixture into the bowl of a 1½- or 2-quart ice cream maker and process according to the manufacturer's instructions. Store in an airtight container in the freezer for at least 2 hours before assembling the sandwiches.

To Make the Sandwiches

1 } Let the ice cream soften slightly so it's easy to scoop. Place half of the cookies, bottoms up, on a clean surface. Scoop one generous scoop of ice cream, about ⅓ cup, onto the top of each cookie. Top the ice cream with the remaining cookies, with the cookie bottoms touching the ice cream. Gently press down on the cookies to level them out. Wrap each sandwich in plastic wrap or waxed paper and return to the freezer for at least 30 minutes before eating.

Pumpkin Snickerdoodle Sandwiches

This is for anyone who thinks ice cream is not appropriate for fall—cold and creamy, with fragrant spices. This'll teach them.

Makes: 12 to 16 sandwiches

Snickerdoodles

Makes: about 2 dozen cookies

2½ cups unbleached all-purpose flour
2 teaspoons baking powder
¼ teaspoon salt
1¾ cups evaporated cane sugar, divided
½ cup nondairy margarine, at room temperature
½ teaspoon vanilla extract
2 tablespoons nondairy milk
2 tablespoons ground cinnamon

1} Preheat the oven to 375°F. Line two baking sheets with parchment paper.

2} In a medium bowl, combine the flour, baking powder, and salt. In a large bowl, cream together 1½ cups of the sugar and the margarine. Add the vanilla and milk, and mix until well combined. Add the dry ingredients to the wet in batches and mix until smooth.

3} Using a cookie dropper or tablespoon, drop heaping tablespoons of dough onto the prepared baking sheets

4} On a plate, combine the remaining ¼ cup sugar and the cinnamon. Using a cookie dropper or tablespoon, scoop out tablespoon-sized dough balls and roll in the cinnamon-sugar mixture. Place on the prepared baking sheets about 1 inch apart. Bake for 8 to 10 minutes, until the cookies have cracked and spread and the edges are set.

5} Remove from the oven and let the cookies cool on the pan for 5 minutes, then transfer to a wire rack. Let the cookies cool completely. Store in an airtight container.

Pumpkin Coconut Ice Cream

Makes: 1 quart

¾ cup packed brown sugar
1 (13.5-ounce) can full-fat coconut milk (not light)
¾ cup nondairy milk
½ cup canned pumpkin purée (not pumpkin pie filling)
½ teaspoon ground cinnamon
¼ teaspoon freshly ground nutmeg
1 teaspoon vanilla extract

1} In a large saucepan, combine the sugar, coconut milk, and other nondairy milk, whisking to incorporate. Over medium heat, bring the mixture to a boil, whisking frequently, then add the pumpkin, cinnamon, and nutmeg. Whisk to incorporate, then lower the heat to medium-low, and stir constantly until the sugar is dissolved, about 5 minutes. Remove from the heat and add the vanilla, whisking to combine.

2 } Transfer the mixture to a heat-resistant bowl and let it cool completely.

3 } Pour the mixture into the bowl of a 1½- or 2-quart ice cream maker and process according to the manufacturer's instructions. Store in an airtight container in the freezer for at least 2 hours before assembling the sandwiches.

To Make the Sandwiches

1 } Let the ice cream soften slightly so it's easy to scoop. Place half of the cookies, bottoms up, on a clean surface. Scoop one generous scoop of ice cream, about ⅓ cup, onto the top of each cookie. Top the ice cream with the remaining cookies, with the cookie bottoms touching the ice cream. Gently press down on the cookies to level them. Wrap each sandwich in plastic wrap or waxed paper and return to the freezer for at least 30 minutes before serving.

Sandwich Fixin's, Fillin's, and Mixin's

Swap out the Snickerdoodles for the Gingersnaps on page 77 for a more intensely spiced experience.

Common Conversions

1 gallon = 4 quarts = 8 pints = 16 cups = 128 fluid ounces = 3.8 liters
1 quart = 2 pints = 4 cups = 32 ounces = .95 liter
1 pint = 2 cups = 16 ounces = 480 ml
1 cup = 8 ounces = 240 ml
¼ cup = 4 tablespoons = 12 teaspoons = 2 ounces = 60 ml
1 tablespoon = 3 teaspoons = ½ fluid ounce = 15 ml

Temperature Conversions

Fahrenheit (°F)	Celsius (°C)
200°F	95°C
225°F	110°C
250°F	120°C
275°F	135°C
300°F	150°C
325°F	165°C
350°F	175°C
375°F	190°C
400°F	200°C
425°F	220°C
450°F	230°C
475°F	245°C

Volume Conversions

U.S.	U.S. Equivalent	Metric
1 tablespoon	½ fluid ounce	15 milliliters
¼ cup	2 fluid ounces	60 milliliters
⅓ cup	3 fluid ounces	90 milliliters
½ cup	4 fluid ounces	120 milliliters
⅔ cup	5 fluid ounces	150 milliliters
¾ cup	6 fluid ounces	180 milliliters
1 cup	8 fluid ounces	240 milliliters
2 cups	16 fluid ounces	480 milliliters

Weight Conversions

U.S.	Metric
½ ounce	15 grams
1 ounce	30 grams
2 ounces	60 grams
¼ pound	115 grams
⅓ pound	150 grams
½ pound	225 grams
¾ pound	350 grams
1 pound	450 grams

Ice Cream Sandwich Index

Ice Cream Index

Cookie Index

Acknowledgments

No cookbook is written alone, so there are many thanks to go around. Thanks to my friends and family for your support, recommendations, and palates. Every author needs good-natured guinea pigs. Thank you to Ulysses Press for being such a great, fun-loving publishing partner for many years now, in particular to Kelly Reed who fields many random, stream-of-consciousness e-mails from me. You handle my crazy with grace. Thanks to the Polar Vortex for making me tough enough to crave ice cream in subzero temperatures. That's Midwest blood for you!

The biggest thanks is to you, fellow lover of tasty things. Whether this is the first time you've seen one of my books or if you followed my long blogging and book-writing journey, thank you for supporting my books and accompanying me on this wild ride.

About the Author

KRIS HOLECHEK PETERS is a vegan baker, blogger, and recipe-formulating mad scientist. She is the author of *The Damn Tasty! Vegan Baking Guide*, *The 100 Best Vegan Baking Recipes*, *Have Your Cake and Vegan Too*, *The I Love Trader Joe's Vegetarian Cookbook*, *Vegan Desserts in Jars*, and the writer of www.nomnomnomblog.com. She lives in the Midwest with her cats where she practices lots of yoga and hoards Bundt pans.